D1301687

Sue Hendrickson

by Karen J. Rothbardt

HOUGHTON MIFFLIN HARCOURT
School Publishers

PHOTOGRAPHY CREDITS: **Cover** © OHN ZICH/AFP/Getty Images. **1** © Louie Psihoyos/CORBIS. **3** Associated Press. **4** © Frank Krahmer/Masterfile. **5** © Louie Psihoyos/CORBIS. **6** B.A.E. Inc./Alamy. **7** © Dave G. Houser/CORBIS. **8** © CORBIS. **9** Ted Kinsman/Photo Researchers, Inc. **10** Associated Press. **11** © Franck goddio/HILTI Foundation. **12** Associated Press. **13** OHN ZICH/AFP/Getty Images. **Global Border** © istockphoto.com/RapidEye.

Printed in China

ISBN-13: 978-0-547-02413-4
ISBN-10: 0-547-02413-4

5 6 7 8 0940 18 17 16 15 14 13 12
4500350925

Table of Contents

Meet Sue

Sue Hendrickson's job is to dig in the dirt. She looks for fossils. She is a fossil hunter. In fact, she once discovered an amazing fossil.

Early Life

Sue was born on December 2, 1949, in Chicago, Illinois. She grew up with an older brother and a younger sister. She was shy, but she loved school. She also loved to read.

She began digging in the dirt and collecting things when she was a little girl. She liked to look for items buried in the dirt, and she started collecting seashells when she was five years old.

After she grew up, one of her first jobs was diving for fish. She was a very good diver, and she used her diving skills to explore sunken boats.

She went to many places to explore boats. In one of these places, she visited an amber mine. She saw amber rocks with insects inside them. One of the insects was over 23 million years old! After seeing these amber fossils, Sue became excited about looking for other fossils.

Amber

Finding Fossils

Sue went to Peru with another fossil hunter to look for whale fossils. They found whale, dolphin, and seal fossils. Sue went back to Peru many times.

On one of her trips, a scientist asked her to help him hunt for fossils in the United States. So she went to South Dakota and worked with his team for three summers.

They visited many cliffs on their hunt for fossils. Two days before they were going to leave, Sue went to visit one last cliff. The rest of the team stayed behind.

An Amazing Find

Sue took her dog and walked around the cliff, looking at the ground. After a while, she saw something that looked like bones. She was very excited. Maybe her dog growled when she made the discovery. She had found three dinosaur backbones!

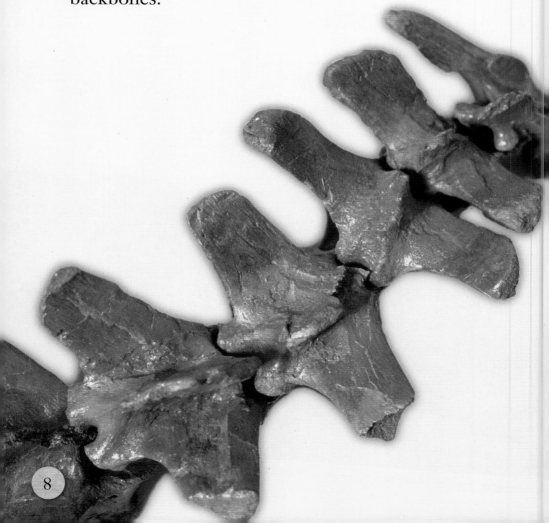

Sue and the team began to remove the rocks around the bones. They used picks and shovels. After three weeks, they were amazed at what they had discovered. It was the skeleton of a dinosaur. It was a Tyrannosaurus rex. They gave the T. rex a name: Sue! Then, they took the bones back to a place called the Hills Institute.

On October 4, 1997, the dinosaur bones were sold to the Field Museum in Chicago. At the Field Museum, it took people over 25,000 hours to clean and put together Sue's bones.

On May 17, 2000, Sue's skeleton was put on display at the museum. The skeleton is 42 feet long and more than 65 million years old. It is the most complete T. rex skeleton anyone has ever found. The museum guards it very carefully.

You can visit Sue, the dinosaur, at the Field Museum. The people at the museum will explain how the dinosaur got there. When you leave, you can buy a great dinosaur souvenir. You can choose from T. rex shirts, toys, books, and more.

After Finding the T. rex

In 1992, Sue Hendrickson began working with a new team. This team was not hunting for fossils. They were hunting for sunken ships. They found a 400-year-old ship named the San Diego. Sue and the team took over 200 tons of sand and rock off of the top of the ship! Inside, they found stone jars, gold, and silver coins.

Sue worked with the team for a long time and went on many dives. This time, she knew the exact spot in which to search! She and the team found gold, silver, and copper coins. They also found cannons, cooking pots, tools, bottles, and swords. Sue was very excited about all that they found.

Conclusion

Sue Hendrickson has discovered many wonderful things. She is still excited every time she finds something new!

Glossary

cliff a rock that extends along a coastline

fossil remains, impression, or trace of an animal or plant

skeleton bones that form the body of a person

souvenir something that reminds you of a place you have visited

Responding

✓ **TARGET SKILL** **Fact and Opinion** What facts did you learn from this book? Copy this chart. On one side write facts that you learned about Sue Hendrickson. On the other side write your opinion about each of these facts.

Fact	Opinion
fossil hunter	exciting
?	?
?	?

Write About It

Text to World Sue Hendrickson studies dinosaurs and searches for sunken treasure. Write an opinion paragraph. Explain why her work is important. What can we learn from it? Be sure to include details in your answer.

✓ **TARGET SKILL** **Fact and Opinion** Tell if an idea can be proved or is a feeling.

✓ **TARGET STRATEGY** **Question** Ask questions about what you are reading.

GENRE A **biography** tells about events in a person's life.